.

Don't Wait Til I Die to Love Me

Vol II

Michael Tavon

Amazon Self-Publishing

Kindle Direct Publishing

© 2021 by Michael Tavon

Other Works by The Author

Fiction

God is a Woman
Far From Heaven

Poetry

Songs for Each Mood II
Dreaming in a Perfect World
Don't Wait Til I Die To Love Me
Nirvana: Pieces of Self-Healing vol. 1 & 2
Young Heart, Old Soul
Songs for Each Mood
A Day Without Sun

Collabs w/ Moonsoulchild

Self Talks
Heal, Inspire, Love

Michael Tavon

Vol. II

Introduction:

First, I'd love to thank you for the tremendous amount of support you all have been pouring into me for the past six months. Even my wildest dreams could never fathom this type of love from readers all over the world. Thank you for welcoming *"Don't Wait Til I Die To Love Me Vol.1"* into your homes and hearts. I hope you love volume two just as much. When you finish, please send me a message on TikTok or Instagram (@michaeltavonpoetry), and tell me some of your favorite pieces. Also, I would greatly appreciate it if you'd leave a review on your favorite book-selling platform too! Also, if you catch any spelling errors or typos, please kindly bring them to my attention at Themiketavon@icloud.com. There's no need to leave a negative review over a few mistakes lol. Authors aren't perfect; neither are our editors; we make mistakes too. Thanks for understanding; I hope you enjoy it.

Michael Tavon

Section I: The Aftermath

A Message to My Ex

Do I ever cross your heart
Like a crucifix?
Was what we had
Real to begin with?

Do your thoughts ever travel
To where we used to be?
Or did you only see me as scenery?
Was I something
to pass the time as you sightsee?

Do you see the joy I found without you
And wonder what could've been?
Do you ever wish for a mulligan
So you can choose me over them?

does your mind ever get
haunted by regret
When you realize
I'm the best thing
you will never forget

To The One Who Still Lurks Their Exes Social Medias

I'm not ashamed to admit
Every now & then
When you cross my mind
I search your name
to see how you've been

How's life after us?
Where have you been
I see you've finally quit that job you hated
cause you were gaining too much weight,
Now you in the gym flexing
on your story
I'm happy for you,

You mostly post selfies
and Geotagged pictures
of the places you always
dreamed of going
You finally see the world
outside of yourself

Oh and
the one you told me

 not to worry about
is now your *everything*
the one who *completes you*
So much has changed,

Us against the world
you wrote as the caption
to the photo of you two kissing,
so cliché

I mean this with the utmost sincerity,
congratulations,
I hope all is well

Michael Tavon

Survivor's Remorse

The blame you carry
Has made your heart too heavy
To beat steadily
You desire to move on,
But your mind is not ready

the clouds in your eyes
pour tears of sorrow
As you beg to the sky
For a crystal clear tomorrow

Dark thoughts haunt
The halls of your mind
You feel so alone
With guilt festering inside

It seems impossible to let go,
When the pain hits so close,
One thing you must know
It's out of your control

The universe is a mystery
Humans can't solve
When life goes wrong
It's not your fault

I hope you realize
before it's too late
Stop hurting yourself
What happened you can't change
It's not your fault,
Sometimes it's just unfortunate fate

Father Cry

In my 30years around the sun
I've never seen my father cry

Not a single drop of remorse for divorce.
Maybe he's immune to heartache.
Or maybe he was relieved to be released
from the shackles of marriage

Mist never filled his eyes
for somber films
& sad novels
while sucking down his sorrow
through 40 OZ bottles .
Maybe, he lived through
too many tragedies
to be inflicted by fiction.

No tears of joy as a proud father
When he watched his children graduate
But he did smile & clap
until his palms vibrated
Maybe, that's his way of celebrating

I've never seen my father cry
But I've heard his laughter a million times

His laughter can be heard
from a mile away.

His deep echoing chuckle
He laughs until his knees buckle
Nothing subtle about his joy

He laughs about his failed marriage
And every wrecked relationship after

He laughs about
his poverty-stricken childhood,
He laughs about the things
that aren't so good

Maybe he never cries
Because he mastered
the art of turning his hurt into jokes

They say
 laughter is the best medicine
Maybe, he's healed through the pain
By becoming the neighborhood comedian

Funerals

The only thing sadder than death
are funerals,
the dark clothes,
sad songs
& Palms full of tears
Feels like rain on a broken heart

Grief is in the air
As death stares back
at you in a casket

Regret from the words
left unsaid boils your tight stomach
like hot water

The person you love
has transcended into a memory
Along with the stories
they'll be buried with
No new moments to capture,
Reaching for laughter
In a dark place

fried chicken, deviled eggs
And green beans on paper plates

Some people weep,
others laugh at old jokes
during the repast.

Sorrow has many faces,
and nothing brings families closer
than death and a hot plate.

Friends at a Funeral

I've made many friends
at open casket parties

The awkward silence
grows louder when you hardly
Know the person being honored

I questioned my belonging,
Being a plus one at a funeral
is far from fun.

But it's how some reconnect
With old friends and distant relatives,

On many occasions, funerals and family
reunions went hand in hand

Weed, cigarettes, and grill smoke
Fogged the air as we gathered outside

I would walk around
& greet people I've never seen before
And forgot their names
the moment they walked away

Elders who knew my face would say
"I haven't seen you since you were knee-high."

The music
The stories
&
Good food
Set the mood

I would even introduce
myself to the person
lying in the casket
and gained a new friend

Over time I learned,
If I really wanted
to get to know someone
Go to their funeral

Grief brings people close
For a few hours
then life goes back to normal

To the Ex Who said They've Changed II

When you take an ex back because they claimed
to have changed, be mindful of their behavior
after gaining access to you. If they fall back into
the toxic behavior that broke your heart too
many times before, they didn't change to heal
themselves. Instead, they lied so they could be
in place to break your heart again.

Daisies

Daisies were your favorite flower
After loving you, I see why
My petals were swept by the wind

You're only capable of loving things
After they bloom,
You never put in the work
to watch anything grow

I was a daisy ~
stem suffocated by your palm
my petals fell off one by one

After loving you, I understand why
I was your favorite flower.

You didn't appreciate my all
And decided it was best to pick me apart.

Once I was bare
With no petals to spare
You moved onto a rose

You killed our love
the way you kill flowers

War

When my intuition and heart
went to war over you.
I was left with nothing
But wounds and question marks

Trophy

I thought love was a trophy,
& I tried so hard to earn it from you

With all the obstacles
you placed in my way
I still overcame

Despite my efforts,
Your heart didn't feel the same
You didn't love me for me
You fell in love with the chase

After all the games you played
I still came in second place

New Home

I left my depression
Back at my birth home
Where it belongs

That's why I often fear
Going back to where I came from

What if we reconnect and talk about
the good ole nights of drinking
Til my stomach became an earthquake

Then continue on about
the many times
Love was a treasure hunt
And I was too naïve to solve the clues

Oh, how we'll laugh about
My precious life like
it was the biggest joke

Then depression will ramble
about the nights
I lost hope
As I fell into the dark rabbit hole

Of being alone

Then we will kiss and
fall in love
All over again

When people ask,
Would I consider going back?
Or
Do I ever miss it?

I say, why would I go back to
A place that never loved me
In the way I deserved to be

Unholy

You made me feel
worth less than worthless
spelling all your curses in cursive
I wondered why I was so drawn to you

With tremors in my stomach
I praised you like churches
While you broke me with no mercy
I prayed for this cult of two

This unhealthy worship
I lost my worth
trying to find purpose In the hurt
When I should've moved on to a new

Menu

I was an option on the menu,
Never your only choice
Shit hurt when I found out
I was competing for your love
Instead of being the only one

To The One Who says They're Afraid to Communicate with their partner

You say,
You're afraid to say what's real
So you cloak the truth
To disguise how you feel
To save your relationship

If expressing what triggers you
Feels like a trap when you speak
My friend that is not love
It's a sign you should leave

To the Ex Who said They've Changed

Good for you,
But did you really change
To grow into a better version you
Or did you *change*
To regain access to me?

I hope you changed to better yourself
Because it would be
a waste of time
 if you did it for anyone else

Closure

Closure is the end of a story
But often, the worst chapter

Love is a novel,
Imperfect, but mistakes are beautiful

We were beautiful
a beautiful mistake

I flip the pages,
And gloss over closure

part of me wishes we could start over
And read between the lines this time

& Part of me knows,
Reading the same story twice
Makes it harder to move on

Instead of closure
Give me an ending that's open-ended
Sometimes cliffhangers are healthy

Allow my imagination
To create the reason why
Our story ends.

Closure hurts more
I'd rather fill in the blanks
On my own

Closure is always the worst part
It's after the climax
And the story unravels
It's where you realize there's nothing to
Comeback from

Turtles

Sometimes strength
looks like curling into a shell
After crying an ocean of tears

Sometimes progress is
small slow strides,
Despite feeling left behind

Sometimes patience
Looks like remaining
calm amid chaos

Life ain't a race
Grow at your own pace

A Message To My Ex II

Despite my best effort,
I couldn't save you
From yourself

My heart, is a warrior,
That fought your battles
For so long,

Everyone knew,
Your brand of love
Was bad for my health

I gave you all of me,
Even when you were wrong

I was drawn to your trauma,
When you flirted with death

Then I realized,
Saving you wasn't my job
To maintain my peace
I had to move on

Michael Tavon

"When grief gets too heavy to carry, poetry is the place you go to feel less alone."

Bridges

Some bridges aren't stable enough to cross
Over & over again
Some bridges aren't worth being repaired after
they burn down
Some bridges aren't worth taking chances on

Bus Stop

I was the perfect bus stop for women
Who waited for their ex
to get his shit together

When he got his shit together
They left me until
He messed up again

When he messed up
they found me where they left me
Sad how they all knew
I wasn't going anywhere

I was the perfect bus stop for them,

they would come & go
They loved the convenience
Of someone being there
Despite being left behind
For someone else

the words your ex wants to say when you find someone new

I hope the happiness you've found,
Makes a home out of you

I hope they provide
a love that fills the well of your soul
Until it overflows

I hope what we had doesn't haunt
Your new life

I hope you've grown from your mistakes
So they won't repeat like your favorite song

I hope the mistakes I made
didn't manifest into a mountain
of trust issues

Most of all,
I wish to you
& your partner
A lifetime of joy

The Apology You Deserved

I apologize for adding another burden to your heart. I lost myself while navigating through my depression and took your time for granted. I thought your love would save me from myself. Instead, I vanished without a trace when I realized commitment was a scary place. I thought I was doing you a favor by pushing you away, but it was the most selfish act I performed. Depression has an odd way of revealing its feelings to the people close to you, and I'm living proof. I never meant to hurt you, but I was too afraid to tell the truth. I had to let you go so I could heal on my own.

Bojack Horseman

For a long time
my depression
was the best roommate
I ever had
it was clean, quiet,
always down to party
and never late on rent

we would drink, smoke, and stay up
'til sunrise
we never talked about our feelings tho

My friends would say,
The living arrangement
was dangerous,
and would harm me in the long run

I told them, *depression* understands me,
and they had nothing to worry about

I treated women like a 9-5
I quit at the first sign of stress
Bouncing from bed to bed
was easier than landing a new interview

Every month, a new girl & a new job

I thought, binge-watching
porn & unprotected sex
was me living life on the edge

After a while
My eyes carried luggage
too heavy to handle alone
My hair grew wild and tangled
like an untrimmed bush
I wore *holey* clothes,
but was far from a saint

People said,
depression was a bad influence,
I always defended his innocence

It wasn't until I started watching
a talking cartoon horse
I realized depression isn't always
loud & angry

sometimes, It's fun, impulsive,
and wears a smile
that make red flags seem wild & charming

Single Life

Being single was fun
until I realized
I was spreading myself
thin like butter to bread

Being single was fun
Until I realized
Trying to find the love of my life
While twisted off long islands
Was like bobbing for apples
In the ocean

Being single was fun
Until I realized
Gambling with my body
Would leave me in a debt
I would never pay off
If I couldn't stop risking it all
For a 20-minute thrill

Being single was fun
until I grew up

18,21,27

When I was 18
at house parties
a guy twice my age
would be there
talking about his heyday

I would always say
"I hope I never turn into that guy."

When I was 21
at college parties
Men in their 30's would
crash the scene
to relive their glory days
and holla at the fun girls
I would laugh and say
"Look at those losers."

When I was 27
In a small hot club,
I hated the music
And the dances
that went along with it
Sweat raced down my forehead

As I got twerked on

I looked around and saw
I was becoming the
The men I made fun of

Michael Tavon

Oil & Water

My parents were oil and water
boiling in the same pot for 13 years

Every other night,
Smoke fumes filled the air
When tempers flared
We couldn't open the windows
To clear the air

They didn't want the neighbors to hear

At a very young age
I knew their love together
wasn't healthy but good
Like soul food

So when they finally parted ways
I was happy

Despite,
their tension being tougher
Than steak well done
The love they had never changed
For their daughters and son

They never punished us
For their mistakes
Momma never kept daddy away
Daddy was poor
but always found a way

Dad had a big ego
Momma had too much pride
But for us,
they did what was right,
When there was a war
between the two
they never made us choose a side

Questions?

How much grief can fit inside a heart before it cracks?

How much tragedy can fit inside a mind before it breaks down?

How much suffering can one life endure before it no longer wishes to move on?

Why must we suffer to discover our worth?

Fatal Marriage

ego and pride are like
the married couple
 that only stays together
Because they're afraid to be alone

One lacks the empathy
to see the bigger picture
While this other is too stubborn
To admit when it's wrong

Issues never get resolved
They just play the blame game,
While performing verbal surgery
Cutting each other open
Until someone breaks down

The two are similar in so many ways
they're practically twin flames
This is why love never sustains
together they remain
Under one roof
But sleep in separate beds

Michael Tavon

Section II: The Mending

Come as You Are II

Come as you are
I promise that's all I need
take off your cool, reveal your heart
to me & take my lead

Come as you are,
honest and gold
Together we'll go far
Love is wild & bold

come as you are
Leave all worries behind
I promise it's not hard
Set yourself free, relax your mind

Come as you are, my dearest friend
Bring the real you, no need to pretend

Type Love (2021)

(after Shi'han type love)

I promise to give that
Sade 'By Your Side ' type love.

That sing love songs
on road trips and cheer for you
no matter how off-key
you are type love

That rub your belly when aunt flow
pays a visit type love.

That create a foreign love language,
so people won't understand
our love type love.

That goofy in public
type love.

*That I'll support your dreams
like a pillow type love.*

That double entendre type love.

That never compete,
but complete type love.

That try to fix things
around the house
even though I can't
work a power tool type love.

That you always believe in me,
so I will always find ways
to make you smile type love.

That "I'll figure it out" type love.
That This is Us,
Rebecca & Jack type love.

That your grandmother
thanking me for making
her baby happy type love.
That make my mother proud of me
for finally finding a treasure
as rare as you type love.

That make my hand
beg me to drop the pen
because it's exhausted
after spending the night
writing about your type love.

Forreal, I want my mind
to create words unheard of,
so I can give love
a new meaning type love.

Most of all,
I know how much of a gift
it is to be loved by you,
so I promise to never do anything
to lose you type love.

Handle With Care III

Be gentle like a babies laughter
Handle with care, you know I'm fragile

I've been damaged,
heart bruised & tampered
hold me softly,
So I won't shatter

Love me like I'm rare
I'll give you my soul, bare

Deliver me from fear
Will you still care?
When lonely calls my name
Will you be there?

Handle with care, my dear friend
Save me from being broken again.

Keep my heart safe
Til the very end
Carry me like petals
In the wind

Mercy

Have mercy on your heart,
Stop tearing yourself apart
Be softer on your soul
You will see the light
beyond the dark

don't succumb to the pain
On cloudy days,
Your eyes will rain
Healing is a long journey
To your brighter days

Clear dead roots
It's time to make room
After all your hard work
your joy will bloom

Mending

May I mend this broken heart with you?
Handle me softly, I'm fragile
too. I trust you with my past
If it's too much to ask,
Feel free to leave 'fore
I fall too soon,
I 'd cry if
I hurt
you

Paranoid

How many people
support you out loud,
but pray for your downfall
These days,
you have more people who claim
to love you
than people you can count on.

your phone doesn't receive
many calls anymore
do you ever wonder,
who throws dirt on your name
when you're gone

Are they really proud
of how you come
on your own
or do they secretly
wish you would fall off

You need to understand
not all *friends* want to see you win

Surroundings

When misery becomes your home, you grow
content with living under the same roof as
despair & disappointment. The space is
uncomfortable, but it's what you're used to, so
you concede to the idea of finding happiness
elsewhere. And you're fine with misery being
your home until your landlord raises the rent.
All because you're afraid to see what the world
has to offer outside of the place that's holding
you back.

Vacation

After working so hard for too damn long
You deserve to find a place
To get away and celebrate your existence

Don't let anyone guilt you into
Working yourself into a grave

You are a human, not a slave.
Give your body the rest it's begging for

Unpack the luggage
under those eyes
and give your heart
the vacation it desires
Slow down, inhale, & unwind

Find a destination
Where you can kick back
& feel young again
It doesn't have to be lavish or far
You can
Go with friends or do it alone

Take this time to regroup
You deserve to be happy
I hope you realize this soon

Here's a reminder

Carrying dead weight doesn't make you
stronger; it makes you tired. Let them go if
they're taking up valuable space & draining
your energy

Gardens

If crops of a garden can't grow in bad soil, what
makes you think you will grow in the city of
misery? Once you surround yourself with love,
the parts of you that were buried in the dark for
so long will begin to bloom.

Anger.

Spiteful people will spend their energy trying to gaslight a fire inside me without realizing anger doesn't live in this temple. My heart is too gold; petty souls will not taint my colorful aura with their dark clouds. As I grow wiser, I've learned I can't control what people say, but I can control how I react. Keeping my peace means more to me than fighting gas with fire.

Influence

Even gold turns into coal
In the eye of the beholder

& Sometimes,
a stranger's reflection
may appear in the mirror

Many people drown
while chasing waterfalls

I've witnessed people lose themselves
while trying to find
Happiness from outside sources

Shapeshifting into the person,
they think the world wants them to be

Once upon a time,
I allowed my interests
to be influenced by peers just to fit in

Until I realized
The gold I held in the mirror
Was beautiful even if I was alone

For Her

She has such a big heart,
There's no wonder why
People are eager to take a piece of it.

Blessing her good grace
To those starving for better days,
Without hesitation

I hope the light she brings to life
Never changes
I hope this cold world
Doesn't turn her heart to stone

Lonely Hour

Even in your loneliest hour,
Through your deepest despair
Always be grateful
For the clouds over your head
And the grass beneath your feet,
Your existence is precious,
And it will go by in a blink of an eye
If you don't find the time
Appreciate this complicated thing called life

Grow in Love

To most people,
love is a dive from the sky ~

As two hearts filled with adrenaline
gracefully descend til they meet the end
Without any chance of feeling high again

To very few love is a garden

Where dozens of seeds were once planted
They never rush the process,
They put In the work to understand

See, when you fall in love
It's a high you'll eventually
come down from

But when you grow in love
New harvest will bloom from the seeds
You planted in the soil

Time is

Time is not on our side
We are young only
for a glimpse of time

We won't let misery
rob our youth
We won't let stress strangle us
like a noose

Time is not our homie
don't get cozy
It will leave without notice

We won't let grief bury us alive
We won't get trapped by our own pride

Time isn't a therapist
It doesn't care about our plans
So let's love each other
 while we still can

5:55

Part of evolving is realizing you're not always right. Part of growing is knowing it's okay to change your beliefs when presented with new information. Being stubborn stunts your perspective. Being deliberately obtuse will keep you from learning the valuable lessons you need to learn

9 to 5 Life

You carry the workload
on your shoulders.
so young, but your body
 feels 20 years older

Beach house dreams with a penny
pinching reality
Dedicated to the *all work,*
no play mentality
The modern-day slave
trapped In legalized brutality

Fueled off coffee
and No Doz
You do a first shift the morning
after you closed
Prayers lost in the wind &
Finger crossing hopes
Waiting anxiously for
approved PTO

grievance cut short
Due to lack of staff
Forced to work sick,
You gotta double mask
Newborn at home,

But Paternity leave doesn't last
They'll watch you
Burn & crash
When you tire out
they replace yo' ass

These jobs will steal your youth,
And gift despair in return
You'll work overtime &
won't receive what you deserve
This is the truth
I hope you learn
Find time to rest your body
There's no need to overwork
Never settle for convenience
Please know your worth
For your mental health
Always put yourself first

Michael Tavon

Art

Loving you feels so natural
is this why the universe drew us together
in pretty hues. There's no darkness between
me & you.

Tattoos

My name tattooed on your heart
So no matter how hard you try
To erase me from your memory
You will constantly be reminded
Of the love you thought
You could replace

A Real Friend is

Someone who never pollutes
your mind with doubt

Someone who never throws
salt on your wounds

Someone who is there
when it counts

Someone who wouldn't sweep
your emotions like a broom

Someone who is transparent
With their intentions

Someone who isn't selfish
With your time

Someone who doesn't treat
trauma like a competition

someone who provides a connection
true & sublime

A real friend is someone who inspire the light
within you to shine, not take it away

Guilt-Trip

When your heart gets too heavy to carry
throughout the day; it's okay to stay in bed. You
don't have to guilt-trip yourself into being
productive. Sometimes the best form of self-care
is doing nothing at all.

Souvenir

Before you exit my arms
Take a piece of me with you
Before the last beat of my heart
Please speak your truth

Treat life like a vacation
Take a souvenir before you leave
Treat each memory like a haven
I hope you find peace after you grieve

Take this moment
As something you can treasure
Take this free token
Memories are priceless forever

Writing is Medicine

It's my therapy,
I feel incomplete when verses
don't flow for too long
I feel lost when metaphors
don't find me at all.

It's my medicine,
I feel weak when
I run out of words to say
Illness takes over my temple
When I don't get my dose right away

It's is my air,
I need this prose
to keep me alive
Without this gift
I wouldn't survive

this is why
I fear dementia more than any disease
A life without imagery and memories
Is a life not worth living for me.

Dear Empath

No more searching for peace
In broken homes
No more fighting to mend someone's
 broken heart
No more trying to fix their emotional scars
No more going to war
For the people who started the battle
No more neglecting the person that matters
No more pretending your trust isn't fragile

No more losing yourself
In this complicated maze
No more working hard for a love
That pays minimum wage
You deserve to discover
The person you are meant to be

Do your heart a favor
Shift the focus back onto yourself
You will discover bliss & good health
Once you stop trying to heal everyone else

My Funeral

If I die young,
Keep the same energy you had
when breath still pumped
 through my lungs

I want the seats
at my funeral to be occupied
by the people
who adore the connection we share

Heartbreak & Dial Tones

I heard the pain shaking in her voice
When I said
I couldn't love her the way
she needed me to.
An awkward silence was my response
As the reception faded in & out
She poured out her heart
Just for me to spill it like water

The sound of a broken heart
Isn't pretty over the phone

She begged me to change my mind
I said *we could be friends*

She hung up, we never spoke again

I Hope You Realize:

 you deserve every all the blessings coming your
way. Don't resist the change, never doubt the
good days.

Victory

The people who downplay your victories are the
same people who would jump over mountains
to feel the joy glowing from within you.

Be Aware

Some people will try to guilt you into being who they want you to be, by dangling your mistakes and older versions of you over your head when they notice your aura rising. Many people won't accept your growth as authentic. So when they say: "you've changed", instead of "I'm proud of who you've become." Take it as a sign that you need to leave them behind.

What if I Told You

Sadness isn't something you hide or run away
from. It's best dealt with face to face. If you
continue to run away it will always come back
to haunt you. To be sad isn't a weakness;
wanting to elude it isn't fear, but the chaos
boiling inside your heart won't simmer down
until you confront the darkness inside you.

Celebrate.

No one has the authority to tell you how proud you should be of yourself. Especially if they didn't put in the work with you or nowhere to be found when you needed their support the most. They watched you struggle without lending a helping hand. So, be loud with your joy. *Some people* only try to humble you when they envy how far you've come on your own. So, celebrate yourself; only you understand the stress you've endured to get to where you are today.

Calmness

There's a calmness in her aura
that settles the storms in my aorta
she provides a sense of peace
I've never felt before her

I love the way she loves
Her heart is a galaxy
filled with cosmos from above
Her goddess energy comes naturally

She is warm like fur
Bright like the sun
She's cool like a *burr*
there's no doubt she's the one

The heart knows what's true
and what my heart wants is *you*

1205 Days and Counting

It's been 1,205 days since
the first time
I said I love you,

The language felt
so natural rolling off of my tongue
my soul felt back at home
after being lost for so long

From day one to day 1.205
Our bond has remained gold
I hope you feel the same about me
Til we grow old

Michael Tavon

Overthinking,

The mind of an overthinker; cluttered with
rainbows & thunder; Loud, bright, & rarely
calm. It's a blessing & a curse to feel what has
yet to come, to be aware and alert. It's good to
think ahead, but it hurts when your intuition
guides you in the wrong direction. Sometimes,
life passes you by when you over-analyze
instead of simplifying; you often lose sleep
while conversing with yourself at night. They
say mediation is the best medication if you want
to slow down a mind that runs 1000 miles per
hour, but it's impossible to be still when you
can't stop thinking about the thoughts you're
supposed to stop thinking about.

Unpack

Unpack your baggage and leave it all behind.
You must realize you can't drag your burdens
everywhere you travel; give your heart the
space to be light. Once you learn the lesson,
your heart needed let the moment pass. There's
no growth in holding on to the baggage that's
holding you back.

Sin

Breaking your heart would be a sin
Because you're the most incredible blessing
Life has to offer

Trust

You spoke in tongues
When it came to being true
Then questioned why
it was hard for me to trust you

I decoded riddles
Just to unravel the truth
I never knew loving you
Meant I had to be a detective too

Conspiracy Theory

You think the world
is conspiring against you
When the truth is
the cup you sip from
is full of excuses
and chased with self-doubt
as you get drunk
the *I can'ts* and *never wills*
that spew from your tongue
Manifest into a life of *never really trying*
you wonder why it's so hard to sober up
The world isn't against you
It never was
It's always been you
Intoxicating your self
With loathing & self-doubt
The more you say you can't
The more you never will

A Reminder

No matter how far you climb from the depths of anguish, there will always be someone who will pray for your downfall once you reach the peak of your mountain.

Misery

Misery loves to visit your happy place
When they arrive, don't let them stay
Don't give them a key
get an order to restrain,
keep them 1000 ft away

Miserable people
wear the biggest smiles
To bring your guard down
Trust your intuition
Sometimes jealousy
doesn't have a sound

Lock the gates
To protect your peace
Keep your happy place
free of negative energy

Fashion Choices

Bitterness is an ugly color
That's why I never wear it
Love is a fashion statement
I don't hesitate to share it

Some envy me,
But I never dress in green
I choose to wear the hues
That exudes the joy inside me

Foolish

I wasn't ready to love you,
But I still led you on,
I admit it was wrong
Forgive me, I was young

Confusion is the enemy
And it got the best of my soul
I wanted the key to your heart
Without making you my home

all the time wasted
life offers no refund
All the apologies won't make up
For the damage, I had done

I understand
why you wish to never speak again
because when you said
you loved me
I thought it would be best
To just remain friends,

Rejection

They say
Rejection builds character,
but no one tells you this
When your heart
Feels like a rock slowly sinking
to the bottom of the sea
& Thoughts of inadequacy
flood your mind until you drown
in your own self-doubt
You begin to convince yourself
Giving up is better than trying,
They don't tell you
Rejection only builds character
If you find the strength
to keep swimming
After drowning so many times

To The One Who Gave Me Trust Issues

Once fractured,
my trust can't be restored
to what it used to be

No amount of apologies
will repair the emotional damage
you inflicted onto me

It takes a lot of pain
to break a heart this big

 how could I ever trust you again?
after so many chances and me
ignoring the red flags

you still found a way
to fuck it up
Like you wanted to sabotage us

Thanks to you,
when I hear *I Love You*
I wonder if it's real

To The One Who Loves Me For Me

I never knew what real freedom was like
until I fell in love with you

You never pressure me
to be perfect because my flaws
feel beautiful to you

You treat my mind
like the greatest adventure
always eager to learn
& explore my soul deeper

I once convinced myself
loving me was a bet
not worth taking
until you went all in and
bet the house on us

the burden of loneliness
no longer weighs me down

Your love is the sky
my wings soar through the clouds for

Michael Tavon

To The One I Want to Grow Old With

I hope our love grows old
with grey hairs and smile creases
around the mouth
So when people see
us walking through the park
hand in hand
they'll see a couple
who spent a lifetime laughing
and enjoying each other's company

To The One Who Means Everything
 To Me

If you could see yourself
through my eyes,
you'd see why I always
see paradise when I look at you.

I see more in you than just scenery,
but beauty like yours
don't come around so easily

You're the compass
my heart needed
I'd be lost if I go back
to a life without you

When I say *you mean everything to me*
it's an affirmation, not a curse

I say these words like a prayer
you deserved to be praised,
and put first

For everything you've done for me
My life will never be the same
You mean everything to me
in the most inspiring kind of way

A DM Love

O how a simple hello from the perfect stranger
can change your life within the blink of an eye

Insomnia

I rattle my feet hoping
the vibration rocks me to sleep
but thoughts of my friend from 3rd grade,
high school crush,
and the stranger I met once
at the grocery store
occupy my mind

I toss & turn,
with my eyes forced shut
Now it's 3:47 am,
my stomach -- begging' for a snack,
& I can't get that one time
Creed played hooky
and caught the same bus
his colleagues were on
to stop replaying

I'm half asleep, wide awake
it's 5 am, random thoughts I can't shake

Cupid's Arrow

When cupid's arrow marked your soft skin
with battle wounds, it reminded
You the big risk love can be
but it's worth the gamble
When you go all in
And strike gold
With the
one

Home Address

You --- where my heart
hangs its hat and
kicks off its boots
after a long day

My heart works so hard to never
be homeless again,
because the shelter for broken hearts
is the saddest place to live

Despite temptation,
my heart knows what it wants
it has no desire
to dream in another a bed

You are a haven, a home without stress
I will always come home to you
because you are my heart's final address

God's Plan

They always say
"God has a plan."
When someone you love dies

That sentiment makes my stomach curl
Grief doesn't care about God's plan
When your heartaches
You just want to understand
Why you won't be able to touch them again.

What type of sick plan involves
The death of someone I love?
Why does someone have to die
For me to learn?

Make it make sense…

Don't tell me, "There's a purpose for
everything."
when most deaths happen
for no reason.
Most of us die for nothing,
But we lose everything

I know these clichés are said
To patch the wounds on a broken heart,
But grief will never be healed
By vague platitudes and overused quotes

A Poem About Nothing

Swinging on the hammock
Under the grey sky,
Cardinals and blue jays
Converse in the trees
A stray cat glares
Likes she's casting a hex on me
My niece presses
her face against the door screen
She Begs to join me ~
My fiancé tells her to take a nap -
But right now
Being alone makes more sense
Phone on silent
I don't answer texts or calls
Sometimes I need my space
&
I won't feel guilty for saying it
Most humans wish for the same
But afraid to appear selfish
So they allow their space to clutter
Until they're driven crazy

We should be allowed
to be selfish a few hours
a day without being judged for it.

Aloneness is gorgeous,
I hope you get the alone
Time you deserve too

To The One Kissed in The Rain

My heart -
knocked like the damn police
I was nervous, to say the least

"Almost there," her text read
I paced in my room
Trying to keep my cool
I didn't want her
to see bullets sweat
For my forehead

God and his angels
were bowling in the sky,
I asked them to quiet down

I layered my armpits with deodorant,
Brushed my teeth,
and released the waste
that boiled in my stomach

I peeked through the glass door
The rain was pissed off for some reason

I went back to my room and waited
And paced from one corner to the next

Until Three gentle taps hit the door
From there, my life changed

When I opened the door,
We were met
with a force of the wind
Surrounded by
darkness and a shower from heaven

She stood,
In her soaked clothes
with a smile that froze time

I grabbed her by the waist
And kissed her
like her lips
Held the cure to sadness

I let her in
Gave her a fresh dry towel
Then undressed
We pressed against each other
For warmth

That night,
We killed the distance between us,
and gave birth to a new beginning

For The Friend Who Needs This

Despite feeling lost
you will find your way
back to yourself

Despite feeling broken,
you will mend your heart
whole again

Despite feeling alone,
you will realize
it's better than being surrounded
by people who create
drama and disruption.

Despite your life
feeling like it's spiraling
with no sense of direction,
you will find the balance
to center your mental.

I hope you realize this
before it's too late
I hope you believe
you're strong enough to survive
the forces that try to break you down

Temporary Highs

We don't stay young forever
So why waste your youth
Trying to make
temporary highs
Last a lifetime

When the joy of the moment fades
Don't fight to hold on,
Move on, make the space
To create new ones

Oysters

My second first love split me wide
in the softest way
she caressed my shell ~
encouraged me to open up more
When I did, the pearls inside me
were exposed,
she began to love me
beyond the surface

When she opened up,
I saw a treasure
no one else saw before
I kissed her pearl
& said, "I'll love you forever."
she let me love her deep
& below the surface

We were two oysters
one a virgin, the other emotionally closed

When the ocean set us apart
she never said goodbye
I was left with a damaged heart

Present

rough palms from years of carrying these
burdens, on this journey of mine
the stress slowed down my progress
I had to choose between
holding myself back,
or letting go
to make space
to be
free

Michael Tavon

"Even when you feel like nothing, you are still whole, complete."

For the People Who Doubt Themselves

You're still learning how to love yourself
without doubting every step you take. Fear
plays such a significant role in your life, you
count yourself out before you even try. You've
built a wall of excuses to make your dreams
seem harder to reach. You keep sabotaging your
growth because you feel more comfortable
settling for *what ifs* to avoid the possible *never-
wills*. You'll never discover the *could be's* if you
keep holding yourself back.

I'm Still Learning How To Appreciate Myself

a work in progress
but still worthy of applause

Far from perfect
But I deserve to be adorned

I have made mistakes,
But I am still a champion

I am not defined by what others think,
I live on my own terms

I'm learning how to appreciate myself
A habit that's good for my health

The 10 people you should let go of:

1) The people who don't want to grow with you

2) the people who don't want to grow at all

3) the people who don't believe in your dreams

4) the people who pick at your flaws

5) the people you can't trust with your back turned

6) the person who betrayed you before

7) The person who only uses you as a stepping stool

8) the person you must dim yourself down for to make them feel secure

9) the person who always try to knock you down when you're feeling high

10) The person holding you back, even if that person is you.

Michael Tavon

Patience

The moment I stopped trying to force things to
go my way, the universe began to reward my
patience with peace. I needed stillness to
discover joy. So I slowed down before I wasted
too much time.

Connection

My soul only craves the kind of connection
that's gold. I don't need any pyrite in my life.
My aura is too authentic to share it with fool's
gold. I've been a fool before and got
disappointed by counterfeit friends and bogus
lovers. If the connection ain't real, then I don't
want it.

Talk it Out II

Silence your ego,
Let your heart speak
This is our chance to grow
Don't turn a cold shoulder to me
Tell me what triggers you
My ears won't judge
I wanna hear your point of view
There's no need to hold a grudge

Trust me, my dear
Your feelings won't become blackmail
If that's your truest fear
Just know, this bond I won't fail

Let's talk out our differences
This time, instead of arguing, just listen

Mixed Emotions

When my heart beats anxiously and my mind
clutters with doubt, I breathe and become still.
Since emotions are fleeting, I let them flow like
the waves of an ocean. In stillness, I've learned
everything doesn't deserve a reaction.
Sometimes it's best to let a moment pass. I don't
want to fall victim to creating long-term issues
based on short-term emotions.

R.I.P to the Old Me II

Before a version of me dies
I give the flowers they deserve
And tell them
"You were everything
you were meant to be."
Before sending them off
To its new home
I tell them:
thank you for teaching me
all the lessons I needed to learn.
Thank you for redefining
 the meaning of love
Thank you for never giving up
&
Thank you for having the courage
To believe in me when nobody else did

Friends

The older you get
the harder it is to
make new friends
and the easier
it is to let old ones go

you know what you want
and tolerate less shit

You treasure your space
and you just want friends
who don't always invade

As you get older,
you don't mind being alone,
you'll lose many friends
and gain even less
you won't even stress
because life goes on

Section III: Other Things

Helicopters

Nowadays, my heart tremors
every time I see
helicopter blades knifing
through the clouds

I Imagine you grabbing
your baby girl for dear life.
With "I love you."
being your final breath
As she transitioned in your arms

I Imagine your heart shattering
At the sight of everyone praying
To God for more life to spare

The helicopter didn't descend
Gently like a feather
Instead, it torpedoed into the terrain
Causing flames to emerge from the grass

Michael Tavon

I Understand Why Snoop Dogg Loves You So Much

The scent you exude when
You're fresh out the bag
Is aromatherapy to me

The texture of your skin
As I break you down
with my fingertips
Brings bliss before I kiss
Those brown sugar lips

I wrap you in a blanket
And tuck you in every night
I blow your name into the air
as you sing sweet lullabies

You have good conversations
Even better taste in food
The laughs we share
Releases all my stress too

you never cause any harm
With you,
 my worries seem so very small
I see why you're best friends
with big Snoop Dogg

Abandon Homes

I wonder what memories haunt
The abandoned homes I ride by every day

What's now a structure of rotted wood
and boarded windows
Was once a home
To a family of 8
Or maybe, a grumpy old man

So much life stored in a house
That's no longer a home

When the people leave
Where do the memories go?

When Lil Nas X Pissed the World Off

They get offended by two men kissing
On television
And say it's the wrong image
to show to children

While kids recite lyrics
About sex and glorified drug addiction
but don't do anything to stop them
From listening

Homophobes are walking contradictions
They claim to protect children
When they really want to push their religion

They curse gays to burn in flames forever
Like their sins are so much better

If all homophobes go to heaven
I'd rather find a loft in hell
I refuse to share a space
with them even in death

The Office

I would turn to you
To bring joy into my lonely nights

Sand would trickle down my hourglass
As I smiled and laughed
misery into oblivion
My heartfelt at ease
With Dunder Mifflin on the television

In a way, you saved my life,
When I questioned if the next day
Was worth seeing
I knew you'd be there to comfort me

They say
laughter is the best medicine
And *The Office* cured my depression

Basquiat

I paint these feelings
In colors for your eyes
To understand

I'm not going to be what you
expect me to be
I evolve with each stroke
Of the hand

I'm an artist at heart
Who is well aware
Of my worth

I will always paint my truth
as you drag
my name through the dirt

My life is my canvass
I paint the patterns
how I feel

No matter what you say
About my art
I keep it nothing less than real

Night Night

The night is so peaceful
When the rain sings melodies
Outside my window

My heart beats in a rhythm so gentle,
As my head rests on a cold pillow
I feel so safe amid thunderstorms

The rain makes the
most beautiful music
To count sheep to

Middle Child Syndrome

Praise the middle child
for being the perfect bridge
between the emotional whirlwind
Of an elder sibling
And the young bratty wild child

The middle child
The least spoiled & the most disciplined
Of the clan she understands,

She has to be big brother's best friend
And little sister's 2nd mother

A job not often celebrated
But she does it to perfection

Always the supporting role
Never the star
But without her, the film
Wouldn't go far

I bet it was hard being the middle child
As each of us grew five years apart

Each child going through
significant changes

during different phases
Was a difficult act to juggle
For our tired & overworked mother
So there's no blame or shame
to be thrown

the middle child always
had to wait her turn
She was loved
But always loved third
But we all made sure
she never felt alone.

Trumpism

Trump isn't Jesus
Why does he get praised
like the most high?

He's not a blessing in disguise
Can he turn water into wine?

What he says isn't gospel
Why do republicans quote him more
Than Christians do the Bible?

Why do his followers curse hell upon me,
Because I don't believe in their cult?
I'm not to converting to trumpism
Donald isn't a God

Trump is not president anymore
I know the truth hurts
It's time to let him go

Cisterhood

Society says it's okay for a woman's
Sexuality to be a maze
until she finds her way
But men can't bend,
we must be straight,
no poker face

A woman's dress code can be
As fluid like the water we drink
But men can't wear soft colors
Like yellow & pink

When a man wears a dress or makeup
His sexuality gets interrogated
Like he committed a crime

This isn't a slight to women
But a knock-on social construct's door
Straight men shouldn't be forced into
in boxes stored
And queer men shouldn't have
to hide in closets anymore

Women Need Guns Too

They get snatched up
Like weeds in a garden,
When no one is around
To hear their cries for help

Whether it be a grocery store
gym or boyfriend's home
They're in potential danger
Wherever they go

There's no safe space for
women to exist
Because they're perceived
As weak, defenseless
By cowardly men

I hear the stories on the news,
Of women going missing more
Than election votes,
With no hope of returning home

Many of these stories
Don't have happy endings
And it hurts,
Then I wonder if her body
would be lifeless
If she had protection

I think,
women need guns more than men
For when a man decides
to go hunting for his next victim
He would be in for a surprise
When she flashes her pistol.

Stillness

They cry: God, *Bring him back to my arms*
as the doors sweep shut, so no one
can hear grief echoing back
hopes of a bright future
halted too soon when
they arrive home
to a sad
empty
crib

Grown ass Kid

The grey that seasons my hair
Says I'm far from a fool
But have a ways to go to be wise
Somewhere in between
mature and childlike
Being 30 is a weird time

I hang onto the cliff
of my childhood
For dear life
I fear I'll grow old
If I let go

I play Pokémon games
After my money shorten
from the bills I pay

I enjoy clouds watching
& Jumping on the trampoline
while buzzed
There are some things I'm too
Stubborn to grow out of

I'm a kid when I want to be
I'm an adult when it's convenient
Young at heart
Old in the knees

I'm holding onto
the thread of my youth
I listened
When my elders told said
'Don't rush to grow up too soon."

To The People Who are Jealous of Other's Success

No matter how hard you work

Some people will feel you don't deserve

What you've earned

They'll watch your every move

And wonder why success

has yet to come to them too

Instead of putting in the work

They get butt hurt over your wins

Sometimes they're strangers

who pretend to be friends

When jealousy paints their soul

Their true will colors show

They never supported your dreams

They wanted you to fail from the get-go

When Kanye said, Having money ain't Everything Not Having it is

I felt it in my soul
When I was broke,
wearing a company's uniform,
for minimum wage
Collecting change to catch the bus,
Being broke was the worst heartache

Between bills & overdrafts
my cash didn't stand a chance to last

It's hard to feel like a man
When you're 27 having sneaky links
In your moms garage

I always thought the phrase
"Money doesn't buy happiness."
was said by a poor man who
Wanted to feel better about his earnings

The cliché is partially true
But when my mouth throbbed
With an aching pain
I couldn't afford a dentist
So I numbed my gums with orajel

When my back spasms
left me stiff like a plank
I could afford painkillers
But not a chiropractor

And when I felt sluggish
Because my diet
Consisted of microwave foods
And one-dollar menus
I knew I needed more money to survive

See, being a human is expensive
And although money
doesn't buy happiness
It sure as hell makes pain
so much easier to deal with

Too Damn Hot

Running for shade
As we play hide
& seek with the sun rays

Saltwater sweat
Stings my eyes
"it's too God damn hot."
Auntie shouts while soaking
Her feet in the kiddie pool

All the kids hydrate from
the water hose
others chase the ice cream truck
down the brick road

while the elders cool themselves
off with newspaper fans

When summer comes to town
We do everything in our power
To not pass out

Validate

I took me a long time to realize
validation from strangers
Shouldn't be my motivation
To change. What others think of me should
never dictate how I enjoy my days.

Yes Men are More Dangerous Than Haters

You will never grow with yes-men in your
circle. They only tell you what you want to hear
To keep their position. Yes-men will enable you
toxic behavior & encourage you to be self-
destructive. They don't dare to say what's real
because they fear losing access to you. Cut these
Yes-men off the way you would a hater; I
promise they are just as dangerous, if not more.
At least haters keep their distance, yes-men are
always close.

Summer Remains

Poppin wheelies on the sidewalk ~
Mosquitoes feast on my brown skin
A cloud of Gnats shroud my face
As I rip through the humid wind

Footraces on the sweltering brick road
Til the friction burned holes
Into the soles of our bobos
Some of us walked barefoot, home

We'd take trips
 to the candy lady's home
& eat hot pickles & flips
(frozen Kool-Aid)
until red dye covered our lips

The simple things of summer as a kid
The youthful days I will always miss

They Say, Black Boy

They say, black boy
Your hair is not good
When it's wild like fire
Spray it with water,
Rake it with a comb
You'll be presentable for hire

They say, black boy
Your hair shouldn't
Touch the sky
It's too high, trim it down
If you don't wish to die

They say, black boy
You look like a thug
With those cornrows
Running down your neck
Cut them off to earn respect

They say black boy,
You look like a tree
When hair swings
down your spine like tree vines
People would be afraid
of you at night

They teach black boys
Our natural hair ain't gold
They say it's happy, dirty, rough like coal

The only way the white world won't
see us as a threat
Is if we mow our hair low & even
Because black boys with good hair
Receive better treatment

Normalize

Not rushing to a power source
When your phone battery
Is on life support.

You'll be fine if you don't respond
to texts on time
Life will move on if you miss
Trending topics on the timeline

If the tension in your hands swells
When the battery life goes red
Put the phone down
& step away
Spend time with yourself,

Spend time
Without the entire world
In your hands

Listening to the Music

The opposite of ignorance is listening ~
A house of music where love
likes to groove & two-step

Love likes to dance
where it's understood~

listen to the people
you're too stubborn
to understand
how beautiful their music is

Ignorance is no longer bliss
it's a disease
when you're too stubborn to learn
listening is the only way
to cure the illness

Love grooves to the music
of understanding
Love thrives
when we all move in unity

The opposite of ignorance is listening
Give your mouth a rest
Give your tongue a break

Michael Tavon

Open your mind,
To create the space
for your ears to listen
Until you're ready to two-step
With the rest of us

The End

Made in the USA
Coppell, TX
25 September 2023

22019773R00090